Wind Echoes

Wind Echoes

Seagulls
are Teardrops
with Wings

SYLVIA SOMERVILLE

To order additional copies of this book, contact:
Xlibris Corporation
1-888-795-4274
www.Xlibris.com
Orders@Xlibris.com
86974

Wind Echoes is Lovingly Dedicated to:

My husband and best friend : Ray

My son and daughter-in-law: Jimmie & Lori Somerville

My daughter: Christine Somerville

My grandsons: Scott and Christopher Somerville

My Mother & Stepfather: Rose & Ron Powell
(Mom is 91 years old Dec. 27, 2010)

Our Best Friends: Ron & Mary Lowe
(Celebrate 60th Wedding Anniversary, May 2011)

Our Very Special Friend: Edward Lenchyshyn

Dr. Drew Girard,
Lorenza Hicks & Laurel Waldick

My N.F.C.V.I. Teacher: Harold Warner

My cherished: Auntie Ann (Anna May Clark)

Our Very Dear Friends:
Wayne & Bonnie Thomson, Kim & Helen Craitor,
Jack & Betty-Lou Harrington, Dave Parsons,
Ramesh & Sujata, Deepak, Rajesh & Rohit Jain

<u>Our Very Dear Friends</u>
Dorothy McDonald, Bernice Allen, Anne Ledden, Ross Finch,
Walter & Margaret Goerlitz, Bill & Audrey Cain,
Carolyn Taylor, Sandy Underhill, Randy White, Marlane Porter,
Steve & Heather Howkins, Bob & Marie Middlemiss,
Margaret Henry, Anthony Mete, Harizona

My oldest brother: Gilbert Pine & Gloria Hoover
My Only Sister: Judy (Bonnie) Foster
Brothers: Richard & Suzanne Pine &
Wayne & Betty-Jean Pine

<u>The Pilot Club of Niagara Falls, Ontario, Canada</u>
Betty-Lou Harrington, Clara Garritano, Claudette White,
Anna Scobie, Jeanette Campbell, Davina Dunbar
Linda Haitos, Eleanor Kerr, Ann Olivier, Kathryn Coombs,
Elizabeth White, Sonja Williamson, Constance Ainslie
Marjorie Douglas, Patricia Dury, Nancy Edit,
Winnifred Branscombe, Patricia Bennett, Irene Elliott

<u>The Village Creek Neighbours:</u>
Wayne & Rory King
Craig & Debbie
Peter & Joanne
Joe and Cathy

<u>All the Village Creek Neighbours on:</u>
Lower Coach Road, Settlers Cove Drive & Old Mill Road

Prologue

Wind Echoes, like the falling leaf, speaks to all manner of men. In Spring, life's spark became a flame. Then Summer winds fanned fire into an all-consuming inferno. The Autumn glowed bravely on, spasmodically fed by fallen leaf and broken twig. And now, midst deciduous starkness, a gloomy ember simmers its hissing last beneath falling snow.

Nellie, the friend this book is written about is a brave woman silently struggling against pain and at the same time, accepting it. Author Somerville met Nellie while travelling in Southern Africa. Together they enjoyed walking safaris where they experienced the wildlife of Africa, "up close and personal". They followed the path less travelled and met the people of Southern Africa in their mud huts and shared their many rituals. Author Somerville and Nellie saw a side of Africa, not many ever witness.

The last few years of Nellie's life, she returned to her home in London, England. Author Somerville visited her in the U.K. and here, they also created memories to last beyond a shadows reach. Nellie joined the seagulls in flight in 2003. If you listen closely you can hear her calling out, touching everyone with love and compassion. Watch the seagulls and remember, Seagulls are teardrops with wings.

This is a book for all those who are concerned about their brothers and sisters of the human race - not only those who may be starving in a distant land, but the person sitting next to you on the bus, in the coffee shop. Perhaps someone you work with everyday. Reach out to them with a smile, a cheerful word, a hug, friendship! A small gesture of love, compassion and concern may be the little boost they need, to make it through another day. Read this book and take a few moments to realize the true significance of life, love and human kindness. Walk beyond a shadows reach and search for the wind echoes.

Grey autumn skies
Silent snowfields
Afternoons
That last forever
Night visions
Distant memories
Of what feels
A long time ago
Tides
Of evenings past

Plaintive melodies
Shoreline lights
Across the sea
Wishes
Dreams
Hopes
We all have had
Once upon a time

The memories of days in my life
When I was young
And life was long
And time was on my side

Alien worlds
Pulsating timeless and free
Night signals
grow and skip
across a cold dark sky
Black and splendid
Lost quality
Tragic sense
A wordless knowledge
not of this world
But somewhere
long ago
A star forgotten
Moon off course
Vanishing deep
into this endless night

Walk with me along the seashore
Aimlessly
amidst the rocks and gulls
We'll enjoy the solitude
and beautiful peace
of South Africa

With cheerful hearts
we'll follow springs footsteps
into fields of heather
and flower strewn beaches
We'll climb a mountain pathway
High up
into the misty clouds
Where problems are far below
And touch
the wind echoes

Seagulls are calling
Streams
are gurgling under a new sun
Sandflowers
are flirting with the wind
and my soul
still knows life's' vigour

We'll wander through summer's
flower carpeted meadows
While the sun enriches our soul
with God's gift
of peace and contentment

We'll drink
the last of winter's tears
from scalloped clam shells
Scatter problems
into seaward winds

Let's sit upon the rocks
beside the sea
amongst the purple sand flowers
and seagulls
and share this season of life

We'll smile
Cry
Laugh
Enjoy life
While listening
to the wind echoes

✎

Season the memories
within the soul
to touch our minds with peace
in times of need

The birds
have migrated to warmer climates
leaving the barren Cape Flats
suffering pangs of loneliness
Harsh winds
Torment the shivering flowers
Echoing an eulogy to summer's sun
The streams
Have ceased their song
Distant hills
Are clothed in winter garments

Light the fire
Nature
Like me
Is tired
Bidding her enthusiasm farewell
With quiet melodies
Passing beyond the wind echoes

✃

Let's sit beside a crackling fire
Because fire
Is the only fruit of winter
Together
Share our inner feelings
Speak of happiness
And not allow winter's cold touch
To creep into our hearts

Can you feel
My forever love and gratitude
Written upon my smile
Engraved in my heart
Flowing in my silent
Invisible tears

Let's drink autumn's aged wine
Sing songs of remembrance
To spring's carefree times
Summer's delightful laughter
And relish in autumn's harvest

South Africa is my soul's treasure
The solitude and wild tranquility
The beauty
Will exist forever
Within the wind echoes

The rising sun burns the mist
From the sky
Leaving a golden blue
I walk
Upon the shore
Between sand and surf
My footprints are erased
By the sweeping tide
The salty breeze
Tosses my thoughts
Ruffles my hair
Bites my cheek

Tell me
If you can
Of a more precious beauty
Greater inspiration for living
Than that found
In a smile

∂

How precious the memories
Found in a photo
The tragic poetry
Of departure
Tears
Of loving friendships
And the waiting for tomorrow
The words of final embrace
Tears of loving memory
And the coming home

Some bygone afternoon
Fading
Into a dark night
Life's candle
Will flicker and die

But memories
Love
Friendship
Are forever

Listen to my touch
Feel the wind echoes

ß

With every sunset
A twilight is born
Forever
A lone seagull
Such as I
Will cry out
With love and friendship

Walking in wild meadows
I embrace
Shivering sand flowers
Along the seashore
I feel the agony
Of lamenting rocks
Anguished seaweed
And solemn driftwood
Friends
Only sensitive hearts
Will understand

A

Always
Feel compassion
On the whispering sea
Within a lone seagull cry
The laughter of meadow flowers
And in the sky's teardrops

Sea waves lashing
the silent rocks
Damp strand flowers
And Seagulls

Night descending
With moonbeams and stardust
Sweeps over my footprints
Receding
With the midnight tide

B

Without God
Without love and compassion
Without family and friends
There is nothing

Tell me of a more precious beauty
Greater inspiration for living
Than that found
In a smile

Listen to my touch
Feel the wind echoes

ⵌ

Sitting silent
In the dying light of sunset
Reflections
Cast upon the wall
The shadows
Of what has come to pass

My soul is heavy
Mind in distress
Life
is quickly fading

The past
Claims the past
Questions left unanswered
And the sun
Continues its journey

ℬ

&

The silent
Lonely struggles
Cancer brings
Sometimes makes
Us twilight people
Abandoned
Yesterdays discarded

Friends
Close your eyes
I'll tell you of a love undying
Of a world
That begins and ends
In searching for the whys

You need only
Look to the heavens
For peace
Comfort
Love

B

ℰ

Grey autumn skies
Silent snowfields
Afternoons
That last forever
Night visions
Distant memories
Of what feels
A long time ago
Tides
Of evenings past

Thoughts warmed by one more gin
Plaintive melodies
Shoreline lights across the sea
Wishes
Dreams
Hopes
We all have had
Once upon a time

ℬ

Tonight
I long to rejoin
The world of the living
But people reject me
Refusing
To let me be a part
Of the living world
Of smiles
Laughter
Life

With the company
Of one last gin
The memory of days in my life
When I was young
And life was long
And time was on my side

ℬ

Alien worlds
Pulsating timeless and free
Night signals
Grow and skip
Across a cold dark sky
Black and splendid
Lost quality
Tragic sense
A wordless knowledge
Not of this world

But somewhere
Long ago
A star forgotten
Moon off course
Planets in lost orbits
Vanishing deep
Into this endless night

A

The dreams
Hopes
The promises
Held within the heart
The tears
Shed in the darkness
No one shares
For the joy once known
And the paper smile
Kept for the world to see

B

℀

I stand
In a patch of wilderness
My home
Body
A vessel
Of weather
Illness and pain
A lonely spirit
Hidden within
My story
A journey
From nowhere to nowhere

I'm a creature
Of desert sand and wind echoes
An element of time
Here I stand
And will continue to
Consigned to a world
Without direction
Without purpose
So turning away
I join the sea
Sand flowers
Seaweed and solemn driftwood

Like the white sand
Beneath my feet
I'm useless
Of no value to anyone

I awake crying
A soul in distress
Full of broken dreams
Sleepless nights
Feeling hopeless
Succumbing to depths
Once thought to be unreachable

A reclusive
Solitary figure
Walking
The empty path of loneliness
But blessed
With the encouragement
Of my friend
At least one
Not afraid to walk with me
Beyond a shadows reach
Behind the wind echoes

&

The pale sun of October
Whispers
About November snows
I tire so quickly now

&

&

The end of another lonely day
Grave markers
Of solemn nights fleeting
I walk alone
Weeping
Under the stars of a wounded sky
And wonder
Will I make it through this night

In times such as these
When the mind
Holds onto yesterdays
Haunted forests of memories
Whisper a last farewell
To a final sunset

Senses lulled by crashing surf
Shadows drift
Amongst a sea
Of comforting thoughts
Misty shores
Slumbering eyes
Drifting
Towards the eternal sleep

B

Far beyond the solitude
Of a sleeping city
Above the stars
The world slips away
In comforting darkness
Silent promises
Hopes
Surrender to defeat

The cold midnight river
Winks out her distant lights
Silence
And the earth sleeps

Listen to my touch
Fading
Too quickly
Beyond a shadows reach
Lost
Behind the wind echoes

~

The spark
That finally detonates
The jettisoned depth charge
The blast
That screams of conclusion
Diagnosis
Cancer

It smashes the ear
With the force
Of a hundred sticks of dynamite
Exposes all façade of reality
Naked
Strips away all traces of tomorrows
Devastates the spirit

It crushes
Destroys
It crucifies
Obliterates
Any remnants of courage
Hope for survival
Cancer
Terminal
The torturous mutilator

~

A

Pain
Sears throughout the body
With unequalled ferocity
It bores deep
Into the spirit
Threads its way
Throughout the mind
Relentlessly rushes
Toward final destruction

Nothing can detract
Nothing can retard
Nothing can lessen
Its staggering wave of devastation
Its irrespirable damage

B

❧

Its remorseless journey
invades the soul
Without mercy
It infiltrates
Infects
Attempts to exterminate

☙

It ushers in unbearable pain
Excruciating
Relentless
To execute its ghastly atrocities
To complete its horrific mission
Manifests the poisons of distortion
Paralyses movement
Inhibits balance
Renders weariness
Exhaustion
Hopelessness
Irrevocable destruction wrought

From this moment onward
There's irreparable damage
A terminal causality
Condemned
Lost
Shattered
Broken and rejected

Forever externally branded
Life from this day forth
Instantly
Irreversibly altered
Never quite the same
A painful
Slow
Lingering conclusion

From the way I appear
In the mirror
To my awkward gait
From the manner in which I drive my car
To the way I sip my vodka
To the manner in which I sign my name
Left to bear the indelible tarnish
Of an incurable
Killer disease

A

The hideous
Haunting reminder
Of that fateful
Singular remark
Cancer
Terminal
That changed and shaped
My destiny

Left like a torn
Discarded book
To live out the days
The remainder
Of wounded sunsets
In a rejected
Lonely existence

B

✑

The smoky dawns of autumn
Winters friendly bite
The songs of spring
Summers cherished embrace
Lost

Forever lost
Until the final hour arrives
That moment of sacred release
The realization
Of spiritual peace

That warm
Refreshing salvation
When my soul leaves pain behind
Discovers
Peace and rest
Within the embrace of conclusion

✑

Standing alone
In the flickering candlelight
Waiting for my God
Tears stream down my face
In the dying light
Of a wounded sunset

Nothing but emptiness
Serene smile
Shadows of yesterday
Lost tomorrows

Silently I pray for conclusion
To release me from this anguish
Relentless torment
Of cancers pain

A

My soul
Is a piece of driftwood
Discarded by the land
And the sea

Alone
Upon this desolate shore
I wait
Like a seashell cupping unshed tears
I wait
Until light merges into darkness
I wait
Until the birds are seen no more
And the seas murmurs softly
Now harshly
Again softly

My cold hands
Clasped around my knees
Shoes
Half buried in snow
I wait

The icy wind blows my hair
Face wet from spraying waves
I wait
Asking why
Why should this be

B

ℐ

The sea overwhelms me
Sweeping doubts and fears away
Beside its overpowering immensity
Still and silent
I wait

A piece of driftwood
Abandoned
Upon this cold seashore
Alone
In this vast world
Of sky
Sea and living

A seashell once full of life
Now echoes
With the murmur of the sea

Nothing is left now but memory
And the salt
Clinging close to my skin

But still
I wait

And dare to hope

ℬ

*I've watched the life of a rose
The birth was soft
Gentle as morning dew
But soon
Rain and winds
Tormented its existence*

*Determined to survive
And smile at the sun
The rose stood firm*

*Defeat
Gnawed within seeking destruction
My heart
Experienced its courage
Struggling to remain*

*Weak and tired
Its head bowed
The stalk broke under the strain
Leaves drained of colour
Drooped
Thorns lost their sting
Life
Dripped away*

Petal following petal
The rose tumbled
Lost now
Somewhere in the weeds

My thoughts drift
Into the density of space
Times past
Words of encouragement
Quiet strength
Distant stars still my tears

Some bygone afternoon
Fading into a dark night
Life's candle
Will flicker and die
But remember
Love
Friendship
Memories are forever

Listen to my touch
Feel the wind echoes

My life began
At the end of darkness
But will cease
Before the morning sun
Tears flow
From my pleading eyes
And are dried
By the touch of love

Today I exist
A lonely
Drifting seagull
Flying on tired wings
Searching for tomorrows sun

A moment of serenity
Lightens the heart
But like a morning dewdrop
Shimmering
On a sand flowers petals
It lasts but a moment
Then is gone

&

Sitting amongst sand dunes
The wind ruffles my hair
Flirts with the strand flowers
And shadows
Thread their way throughout the dunes
And vanish into the sea

Who can know peace
Without first
Having tasted tears
And listened to a raindrops story

Who can know friendship
Without first
Having felt a rebel wind
And experienced deep loneliness

Sharing laughter with meadow flowers
Listening to cheerful sunbeams
Holding the hand of a friend
Therein lives true happiness
Experiencing our balance
Of smiles and tears
Shared within friendship

&

The sun
Not long ago
Held its flaming head erect
Refusing to surrender to days end
Without a struggle

The clouds
Lashed out in annoyance
Your time is ended
Old sun
New always replaces old

The heavy clouds
Enveloped the sun
Choking all life colours
But still
The sun refused to die
And resisted
Until the clouds blackness
Smothered
The suns last breath of life

The pale moon is full
Too soon the sorrow
Of the suns death is forgotten
Too quickly
I feel
And my soul cries for those
Who did not enjoy
Or experience
Its last moments of splendour

How easy it would be
To forget life
How easy it would be
To surrender
Accept conclusion
Cry sun
For you are no more

Each day of life
Is a precious gift
Wrapped in bright sunshine
Tied with delicate dewdrops
And sealed with the rains teardrops

Each moment of life is unique
Lived but once
Friends
Listen to my touch
Search for the wind echoes

My soul is heavy
Knowing soon
I must say good-bye
Thanks for walking beside me
Beyond a shadows reach
And sharing your encouragement
Compassion
Understanding
And friendship

My heart feels deep sorrow
As I watch the sunrise
And wonder about the sunset

Good-bye to the story upon the waves
That echoes throughout the trees
And splashes its lament
Unto cold grey rocks

Friends of my heart
From heaven
My love will paint a sunrise
Blazing with happiness
And a sunset
Of wounded tranquility

My soul will always exist
In laughing meadow flowers
In the warmth of giggling sunbeams
And within the lonely
Peaceful cry of a gull

Listen to my touch
Walk behind the wind echoes

Hope
What is hope
Radiation
Chemotherapy
Drugs
And the pain
Always the pain

How do I cope
How do I fight for life
Should I give in to conclusion
Is life to be constant pain
Rejection

So much to accept
No one to lean on for support
So much unbearable pain
No one to give me hope

Where is the fairness in life
Lord help me to help myself
Give me understanding
Help me fight for tomorrow
Stay with my soul
When its time to depart this earth

Rain
Is for memories
Snow
Is for sleep
Tears
Are for yesterday
Hope
Is forever

Touch my heart
With a memory
To echo forever in my soul
To comfort
To strengthen
For the difficult days ahead

Raw blasts of winters bite
Turns the faded earth brown
Lamenting trees stand naked
Skeleton remnants
Of summers warmth
Shivering now
In loneliness

Friends
Draw hearts closer within
Touch peace
Understanding and compassion
Share sorrow and happiness
Before nature paints the frosty air
With life's sunset fire
And extinguishes a soul's
Earth existence

ƎI

Slide down memory's cascading highway
Pass drifting dunes
Amongst the mind's sandcastles
And stream into endless flight

Along rivers of molten gold
Feel the cool refreshing waters
Tumble you into deep recesses
Trail off behind the sun and moon
Fade into the wild twilight
Listening to the wind echoes

A full moon
Cast the shadows of night
Cruel gales
Probe in contemplation
Of laying waste
The gardens of life
My soul experiences
sensations of conclusion
Awakening from treatments
Afraid
Alone
I cry

ß

My eyes wander around the room
Longing to penetrate the ceiling
See the stars
The moon or sun

I feel despair without words
Hopelessness
Pain
Pain beyond my power to comprehend

Seized with an immense loneliness
Isolation and deep grief
My soul cries out for a touch
A word of friendship
Closeness and support
But loneliness becomes a crushing thing
An illness of the spirit
A desperate
Bottomless need

Silence
Emptiness
Wild grief
A sense of dreadful loss
Fills my soul
Death embraces a warm heart
I experience terror and sorrow

Weakness and unbearable pain
Cause my soul to long for surrender
But stubborn determination
Gives me the strength to fight
Not to accept defeat
The soul must never give up
Its right to sing
Echoing the beauty of life

Closing my eyes
I drift on a dark
Agitated sea
Nothing matters
Nothing but death
But I dare not give in
To this treacherous
Betrayal of will

Alone
It feels like a gash
Has been inflicted to the heart
A lion
Has ripped out a piece of my soul
Sad music
Within the core of myself
Emphasizes loneliness

Sea waves lash the silent grey rocks
Damp sand and seagulls
Mesmerize the night
Descending amid moonbeams

The cold winter sun
Filters down through grey clouds
Unto this desolate field of naked
Skeleton trees and dry straw
My soul is empty

Listen to my touch
Feel the wind echoes

A memory
Forever treasured
Revitalizes
Inspires and comforts
Longer than forever

ℐ

Long walks along the seashore
Lazy
Dreamless
Timeless
Sea waves crashing upon the rocks
Damp sand and seagulls

Night dropping amid moon beams
While stranded starfish wait
For the swollen
Midnight tide
Warm soft breezes
Tangled seaweed and endless peace

The mind is drunk
Within the stars of a tropical sky
Love
Friendship
Solitude
Are the heartbeats rhythm

ℬ

A gypsy moon awakens
Low on the horizon
Shrouding the world
In golden tides of sleep

It is there
In the absence of light
That hopes
Are strengthened

A gull
Rises from nearby grasses
Soaring upwards
His song
Is a penetrating message

Tears tumble to the beach
Mingling
With the tide and the sea
My soul bleeds
Within the wind echoes

The gull
Makes inconsistent motions
Descending lower
With each windy blast
He looses height
His effort useless
He's grounded

Pacing
Unsure
Of how to defeat the gale
He waits
Testing the wind
Again he rises
Apprehensively
Then unhindered
by the raw elements
Flight successful
His music is
Composed by angels

It hurts
To realize
What the eye sees
Can never
Be fully expressed
What the heart feels
Can never
Be captured
With mere words

Some bygone afternoon
Fading into a dark night
Life's candle
Will flicker and die
But memories
Love
Friendship
Are forever

Listen to my touch
Feel the wind echoes

With every sunset
A twilight is born
Forever
A lone seagull
Such as I
Will cry out with love

Today
The valley of death
Feels near
God stay with me

My soul cries out
Seeking comfort
Oceans can't stop heart feelings
Comfort comes

Life is fading
Treatments
Drugs
Seem useless

The pain
Threatens to reduce me to death
The last fragments of life
Are ripped from my soul
My will
Is crushed into dust
Life is too painful

Desperate need for a hand to hold
Understanding and warmth
But there's no one

My heart cries out
Spirit weak
I shiver with cold
It's difficult
To show a paper smile

Deaf ears
Hear not the anguish
Blind eyes
See not the suffering
Cold hearts
Feel not the defeat and loneliness

∂

Time
Is a hot sun
Mirrored
Upon a glass sea
Shimmering
With illusion

ß

ℰ

Pain
Nothing but endless pain
Cough
Threatens to steal breath
Someone
Please awaken me
Help me before cancer
Reduces me to death

Afraid
Eyes search a dark room
Need another heart to share

Silent
Lonely room emphasizes
Hopelessness
Smothering pain crushed spirit

Without support
Without someone to share
To understand
I'll never awaken
I'm afraid

ℬ

A

Beside the fireplace
I sit and reminisce
Thoughts turn to South Africa
The beauty and solace
So infinitely lonely
I'm reminded of the braii
Vodka and friends

Walking alone
Beneath the stars
Of a falling sky
A lion roars
Announcing the coming dawn
Wandering somewhere
Beyond the distant hills

B

Can there truly be
Any greater perplexity
Of wonder
Than reality

Listen to my touch
Search for the wind echoes

Clouds of rose cobwebs
Drift around a blazing orb
A lone seagull
Wings touched with sunsets glow
Sails upon the horizon
The sea and mountains
Reach up
Blending softly with the night

Threads of silver rain
Refresh fields of wild flowers
Thirsty meadows laugh

Trees
Spread their dry branches
To catch
The clouds healing raindrops
Echoing thunder announces
The storm

Soon
Splendid rainbow hues intensify
The tempest end
My soul merges with the sea
And drifts with the seagulls

Evening
Draws the sun
Into an orange ball
Darkness comforts
The moon smiles
Stars beckon me
And with a wink
The sea races onward

Shadows of naked trees
Invade the waters surface
All disturbing human elements
Melt beyond awareness
A longing loneliness
Fills my heart

Tender winds
Blow a mist across the stars
Feelings of anguish
Lostness
Pure grief
Only nature shares
The cry of my soul

A dying sun hurls spears
Of amber light
Waves
Surge ivory and jade
Pure grief subsides
Loneliness closes in
Like a soundproof wall
I see the faces of people
Perceive their words
Gestures
But feel no touch
Hear no words

Along the seashore
I discover a seagull
Battered and sick
Shivering between boulders
Dying
Nothing can restore it's life

Gently
Placing him on a grass bed
I shelter the seagull
From the harsh winds
I cover him
With dry straw blankets
Stroke his tiny head
And pray
For his departing spirit

No one
Should suffer or die
Alone
Forgotten
Unloved

ℰ

The impact of death
Pain of reality
Renders anguished tears
The sun has left my heart
Leaving only glaring lights
On a crude
Backdrop of existence

Vitality
Colour and joy
Subsides into a wasteland
Of choking sand
Defeating the struggle
Inspiration
Courage to continue

What is life
If it offers only loneliness

ℬ

Torturous burning
Radiation
Mountains
chaotic and tumbling
Rise in a grey mist
Oceans of flame
Whirl me dizzily
Away from reality
Searing
With incandescent rainbows
Flashing
Over bottomless depths
Of pain

Seeking escape
My thoughts recall
Mauve twilight
Weaver birds
Peace
Silver drops of silence
A peacock sings
Within the dimness
Of an unseen wood

It hurts to realize
What the eye sees
Can never
Be fully expressed
What the heart feels
Can never
Be captured with mere words

Blue twilight rain
Fragrance of wet Bluegum trees
Shaking crystal drops
Of silence
From bowed heads

I finally collapse
Breathing painful
Laboured
Pale with apprehension
Drained of strength
I long to sleep

Friend
Take my hand
Share the thoughts of my soul
Help me find the strength
To continue the battle
Stay with me this day

Listen to my touch
Search for the wind echoes

A

Sea waves
Lash silent rocks
Sand flowers
Seaweed
Night descending
With moonbeams and stardust
Sweeps over my footprints
Receding on the midnight tide

Last night
I saw your face in the sunset
Your eyes
Were bright with tears
Someone had stolen your smile
In that moment
I wished I was able to reach out
Draw you near and dry your tears
Replace your smile

B

𝒜

Days are long
Since we said good-bye
Wine and beer
Pebbled beaches
Words left unsaid

Parting smiles
The wave good-bye
Your sparkle felt
The plane fading
Into horizon mists
Magical scent of clouds
As I slide back
Into long sunset memories

Beyond Cape Point breezes
Sun baked sands
Beyond cooling waters
Aloe
Arum lily and protea
Solemn Baobob trees
Beyond distant mountains
And roaring lion
There is always you

ℬ

The dreams of a lifetime
Illusions in the moonlight
Visions
Plans to ease suffering
Ageless
Forever lost

Moments shared with the sea
Gulls
My heart touching
The cresting waves
And feeling
The stars teardrops

Friends
Relax amongst strand flowers
Experience lamenting rocks
Anguished seaweed
Solemn driftwood
And realize the briefness of life

The sea forever sings
Forever sorrows
Grows weary
But never dies
Our friendship
Is a forever sea
Touching the soul with love
Compassion
Understanding

Friends
Are the hearts special warmth
Like a chestnut sunset

Listen to my touch
Reach out
Search for
And feel the wind echoes

Beyond a mountain pass
Shimmering in ageless sunshine
Lost horizons
Nestled in dark folds
Of evenings past
Days of purpose
Lies my special place
Em-Tandeni (Place of Elephants)

Serene bay of soft ocean tides
Thundering surf
Majestic solitude
Ancient moonlight
Plaintive melody
Of singing children
Hungry natives

Rasping baboon
And lion
Are captured
In memory's sandcastle
Waiting
For the morning sun

Some bygone afternoon
Fading into a dark night
Life's candle
Will flicker and die
But memories
Friends
Are forever

Listen to my touch
Feel the wind echoes

The sunset storm
Has rumbled past
Shoreline lights
Outshine the stars
The moon swells the tide
Night melodies
Drunken the senses

Standing alone
At Blouberstrand
The hot morning sun warms my face
Salty
Unharnessed Atlantic gales
Rip into my sad heart
Knowing soon I must leave
Beautiful South Africa
And my dear friends

Table mountain
Sheds tear clouds
Drifting down her slopes
Touching my soul
Relating her farewell

My soul cries
Farewell South Africa
Land of mysterious beauty
Intense character
Unyielding voices of anguish
That echo amongst sand dunes
Throughout mountains and karoo
Resounding the intense emotions
The severe turmoil
Of the lands' birth with rebirth

This morning dawned as others have
The stars grew dim
Shadows faded
An invigorating sun
Scampered across a drowsy sea
And crashed
Upon the misty shore
Spraying sand flowers
With mischievous
Giggling sunbeams

The tide gathered strength
And with a tremendous yawn
Heaved itself upon the rocks
Jarring all traces of sleep
From their soul

Once more
The world has awaken
With its balance of smiles
Tears
Anxious to experience
This splendid new today

A

My heart awoke this day
Heavy with saddness
My soul bled tears
Because soon I must leave
South Africa
Only night's silence
Will feel the anguish

No longer will my steps
Echo
In her mountains
Nor will my eyes
Laugh
In her sunshine rain
My ears will long
For the melody of her surf
My soul will crave
Her wild tranquil solitude
My friends

My heart will no longer
Greet the day saying
Good morning Table mountain
Or watch Eucalyptes trees
Clinging to her slopes
Graciously bend
To let sea winds pass

In the midst of my lament
A laughing sunbeam
Bounced up from a sand flower
And tapped upon my heart
Cheerful and sparkling
With life's wonder
My soul could naught
But feel tranquility

South Africa
Transkei
Em-Tandeni
Friends
You're a part of me

Your mountains and strand flowers
Elephant and lion
Anguished
Suffering
Yet still friendly natives
Your peace and wild tranquilty

Soon my soul
Will watch another dawn
From the shores
Of my Niagara River
In Canada

A

Forever
Time
Life
Emotional seas
Will separate us
But my soul will always
Walk
The wild coast at Em-Tandeni
Experience
The mystery of Table mountain
Wander
The Drakensberg summit
And soar
Wild and free
Within the solitude
Of a lone seagull's cry

B

How precious the memories
Found in a photo
The tragic poetry
Of departure
The tears
Of loving friendship
And the waiting for tomorrow

The words of final embrace
The tears of loving memory
And the coming home to wait

But with every sunset
A twilight is born
Forever
A lone seagull
Such as I
Will cry out with love

♫

Some bygone afternoon
Fading into a dark night
Life's candle
Will flicker and die
Friends be assured
Memories
Love
Friendship
Comfort
Are forever

Listen to my touch
Search for the wind echoes

Seagulls
Are teardrops
With wings

♫

A

Yesterday
I ambled through gardens
Forests and seashore
Always feeling
Their mystical aura
As if something special
Marvellous
Was waiting
Behind the wind echoes

Today
The shadows in the forest
Blend
With the shadows in my heart

Always my soul
Echoes unspoken
Unanswered questions

B

Love
I put such faith in it
Faith
Is it not a part
Of love and trust

Thoughts take frantic flight
Wanting death
The only escape
From this prism of pain

Philodendron droop
Fall limp
Ivy leaves yellow and die
I plead with them
To perk up
But like my hope
They died

The wind hustled
Across the fields
Scraped
The skeleton branches
And whispered
Of death and dying
Around the window cracks
It howls and moans
Sobs
And seeks all ways
To make the end of life
More obvious

𝒜

My mind seeking to escape the gloom
Recalls beauty
The sun falling on the petals of a rose
Light shining through tree leaves
Revealing the tender veins
Baboon scampering through Fever trees
A lion drinking beside the Usutu River
Elephant trampling
Through the Tsitsikama Forest
And Table mountain
Bidding me farewell

I'm usually optimistic
Cheerful and hopeful
Helpful and understanding
So why
Is my strength now frail

Again
Radiation
Drugs
Pain and more pain

ℬ

SI

Friends
I need you
But you're so far away
My heart feels your spirit
Comforting
You're with me always

From life to phantom
As death lay in ambush
Struggling to awaken after surgery
Friends
Help me live
Support
Love and understand
I need you

My voice sought its' echo
My eyes searched
But lost the light
The light
Lost its shadow

ß

ℐ

I felt darkness
Without substance or skeleton
Timeless
Balanced it seemed
On the brink of life and death

Freezing cold
Whiteness
Spinning wildly
Through black nothingless

My eyes lost their blood
Blood
Lost its odour
And the air lost its taste
Emptiness

ℬ

Anguish
Solitude
Smothered my cries
My heart screamed for someone
Anyone
To hold me
And not allow death to take me
Behind the wind echoes

Arms reached out to me
Warm
Strong arms embraced me
With love
Understanding
Support
But still
I was held captive
In the inner-spaces of in between

Face to face with death
A cloud of fragrance
Hovered around us
It took me into a dark cavern
Smelling of mildew
Full of flickering shadows
Empty of meaning
Like stones without moisture

Your smile warmed my soul
Your love embraced my heart
Your words of encouragement
Flooded into my soul

Strength
Grew from somewhere
Unknown
Not yet discovered
An untapped resource
Of endurance
Courage

A

Drifting
Through inner-space of nowhere
I suffer an unquenchable
Thirst for breath
Gag
Choke
Desperately try to breathe again

Somehow
I'm walking the wild coast
The native children
With autumn eyes sparkling
Shouting cheerful greetings
A lion roars
And I smile

I gaze up at shadows
Concealed in the trees of time
With tangled silence

B

Drugs wear off
The dark room enclosed in glass
Machines
Oxygen
Blood
Life
Wonderful life

Long days
Breathing in sharp painful spurts
Die on wings of silk cotton
Clouds drift passed
The unthatched roof of humanity
Spreading a sun-etched mesh
Across the twilight sky

Pain cannot blind
The visions of the heart
Oceans cannot separate
The closeness of friends

❧

The afternoon sun
Twists down
Shooting darts of sunlight
Through the trees

Let strong winds
Carry phantoms into tomorrow
Winds to hang
On naked deserted trees

The end of all things
Is eternal
Shield my aching eyes
From the suns glare

☙

My life has been blessed
I've witness awesome sunsets
In a wounded sky
And sunrises
Shooting darts of hope and joy
Into the new day

I've watched the winds
Sweep across meadows
And have touched
The wind echoes

I've watched dark rain clouds
Scurrying away
And longed to hold them
To make them rain
Upon the roots of withering trees

My heart has touched
The gauzy prism of a rainbow
And longed to bend it and make it shower
Happiness and love
Upon the lamenting
Anguished
People throughout the world
And ease their suffering

Music
Within the core of myself
Threads slow-spaced words
Amber beads of silence

Clutching at twigs that snap
Clouds that dissolve
Dry petals that drop
I cling to life

Ebbing tides drain strength
Ink spreads
Throughout the dark sky

Hopelessness
Makes me feel
Like the face of the sun
Falling helplessly into the sea

Time is writhering
Wind blows dry leaves
Grasses
Sun-bronzed and bent
Hues of dryness
The ghosts of a life that was

From physical being into spiritual
Behind the wind echoes
Does death hold forever slumber
In darkness
Or sunshine warmth
Illuminated by millions of fireflies
Touching loved ones left behind
Seagulls
Seashore and solemn driftwood

*

Winter gales
Bring long hours
Without dimension

The seashore
Touched with frail white lights
And carpets of purple and yellow
Sand flowers
A pale green mist
Peeking
Through awakening trees

Pain
And more pain
Give me relief

Sometimes it seems
I can reach out
And touch the fingers of death
Feel its texture
Experience its grief
Joy
And a knowledge of mystery

*

Yesterfontein
The fields are adrift
With exquisite white flowers
Trees softened
With tangled green gauzy branches
All the earth smells of sweetness

My mind
Always involved in beauty
Nature
Looking at the sea
I project myself into it
Become a part of the sea

I feel the content
Imagine the blue-green universe
Living beneath the surface
Wonder about the fish
Seaweed
Coral
And marvel
at the unknown mystery
Of existence

Watching the gulls
Their wings ignited
With colours of the sunset
I ponder the sun and moon
And their journeys

How deep the hurt
Within the heart
No one shares
I feel so alone
So dam alone
Lost and unneeded

Finally
Realization
Suicide
The only answer

Life is a pain filled hassle
I'm useless
A discarded remnant of life
I don't understand
Why
Because cancer makes me ill
Unable to continue as before
Why do people and life
Treat me different

I drive to the Niagara River
It's ashen grey beneath the night sky
The current boiling swiftly
Towards the brink of the falls

Mans knowledge splashed
The rushing water
With supernal loveliness
Dying cliffs and cataracts
With flaming streaks and tender blue
Rainbow hues
Descending along the surface
Sinking to the churning river below

Gusts of astringent wind
Chill me
Burning tears blind my eyes
I need someone desperately

A

A quiet peace
Dims
Life's painful burden

Too quickly evening is dying
Heaven and earth are reluctant
To surrender this glory
And my heart wonders
How you managed to cast your love
Upon the sky and river
To paint the wondrous colours
For my pleasure

My face rimmed with cold
The sky silent
Echoing with light
And I feel
Hope

B

The nights rapture
Stars and moon
Elements of natures glow
A soundless mirror
Reflecting from the heart
Not to be expressed
With mere words

The cry of pain is stilled
By peace
Your presence vanishes fear
Renews hope
Life's soundless shadows
Shout
Within the wind echoes

I feel the substance of life
Despair
Feel the air
The movement of the stars
And the touch of your soul

The thin skin of evening
Scatters shadowed hours
Like harvested grapes
Sheltered redness
Of the centre of the sun
Falling hopelessly into the sea
Lost behind the wind echoes

Long endless days of pain
Silent
Motionless hours
The wheels of the seasons
Revolving
Always in greyness

Morning
Noon
Night
Only paler or brighter shadows

Sounds approaching and receding
Falling away
Like voices in a drugged sleep
Muteness
Heavy on the tongue
Dryness in the throat
Dimness in the eyes
Loneliness in the heart
Nightmares of demons
And angels

Doors opening and closing
Along endless corridors
A weariness
Loneliness
But at least still blessed
With my friends
Not afraid to walk beside me
Behind the wind echoes
Beyond a shadows reach

Beside the river
I seek the wind
Feel it on my face
Feel alive again

Desperately
My soul longs for life
Perhaps the seasons of my life
Have climaxed
And departure time is near at hand
Perhaps
It's time to walk within
The wind echoes

A

Peace awaits the soul
Beyond a shadows reach
Drifting
Within the whisper of a star

Many nights
I sit in the darkness
Watching
The moons silent journey
Across the starry heavens
Until its demise within the dawn

A train whistle echoes
Along the rim of sleep
Forlorn and lonely
Quickly fading
Resounding
The wails of a lifetime

B

My thoughts return to Em-Tandeni
With its wild tender sea
Unharnessed winds
That blast the dark of night
And scurry out to sea at dawn

Clouds explode
Throwing down rivers of rain
Soon
The sun
Peeks through cracked clouds
Winds soften
Fall limp
And a slow calm
Smothers the earth

Gurgling streams
Lend voice to the mountains
Winds toss the clouds
Scrubbing the hills
With a blanket of mist

The stars are touchable
Along the wild coast
At koffee bay
The sea whispers
The hidden secrets of the moon

&

Atop Table mountain
Wandering through Protea
Thorn and weak-kneed trees
My soul looks down upon a city
Too preoccupied with itself
To care about the starving
Dying
Rejected people
Struggling for existence

Moonlight filters
Through evening darkness
Moths tick off an arc of light
Life passes
Wanes and ebbs

The tide surges
Curls back and pounces
Upon the mind's sandcastles
Washing them away
Sending drifting thoughts
Into a litany of confusion

ℰ

Recognition
Pain
A time of learning
A season of growth

ℬ

𝒪

A curlew calls in sleep
Far up river
Where night casts off her darkness
The Knysna mudflats hump
In the bays warm jaws
Crying gulls drift in

Too early yet
For prawn diggers
The sun drowsy from sleep
Pauses below the horizon
While gulls announce the dawn
Somewhere
An elephant yawns

Life
Is withering
The winds
Scatter the leaves

ℬ

ℐ

I stand under the trees
Overhearing secrets
Of the cold dry wind
Scraping the skeleton branches
Grasses tinted straw-gold hues
Of dryness
And the ghosts of dying hopes

Some days are longer than forever
Burning with sharp pain
Closing my eyes against the torment
I lay in silence
Trying to understand

Today I walk upon frozen meadows
So lightly
The grass won't feel my footsteps
So swiftly
The wind echoes will fill my heart
With peace

ℬ

Em-Tandeni
Long tassled elephant grass
Resounding with the soul of Africa
Acacia and Fever trees
Banyan
And scrub bush zipped with thorns

Rasping baboon and yawning lion
Weaver birds and sun beetles
With sharp clear voice
Drifting within the shadows
Only paler forms of African sunlight

Protea
Dancing in the sunshine
Pineapples
Dripping with mountain mists
Flaming aloe and quaint Baobob trees
Echo with the soul of Africa

ᗝ

Listen to my touch
Walk behind a shadows reach
And search for the wind echoes

With every sunset
A twilight is born
Friends be assured
Forever a seagull
Lonely as I
Will cry out for love

Seagulls
Are teardrops
With wings

ß

Alone I walk briskly
Over crisp brown grasses
Shuffle through dry crackling leaves
Crunch across ice crusted snow
Happiness
Solitude
An inner tranquility discovered

Because of friends
My shield is dissolved
Again I allow myself
To be vulnerable
Let faith and hope
Resurface

Thank you friends
For listening to my touch
And feeling the wind echoes

❧

Hope had become a cobweb
Easily torn into shreds
Love and trust was lost
Somewhere in yesterday
Or waiting
Somewhere in tomorrows

You restored the spark of hope
With your understanding
Compassion
Love

If only people could realize
The terrible loss they suffer
By not loving
Understanding
Showing compassion
For others

❧

How empty and impoverished
Life must become
When the eyes are always turned inward
Upon greed and selfishness
And an unloving attitude

When one does not see
Understand or love others
One does not see
Or feel life

Their soul knows only emptiness
A dry fountain
In a wilderness of bleached boulders
A dead garden full of blowing straw
And skeletons of blasted trees
They become stone
A soul without
Beginning or end

If there's a hell
It is probably filled
With the bitter waters
Of self-seeking egotism
Bruised and bleeding hearts
Suffering
Icy cold emotions
Lacking
The warmth and healing of love
Compassion and understanding

Friends
Show compassion
For those who inflict pain
Cruel words
And try to understand

They suffer unknown anguish
Deep inside and they need love
Support
So they may also find peace
And tranquility

My heart was heavy with sadness
Before my friends touched my soul
Today new strength laughs
At the shackles of pain
Because love and friendship
Are stronger than pain

I'm a tree grown in the shade
But for today
I stretch my branches
Enjoying beauty and friends
While I still have life

When death comes
Let our friendship and love
Be like the fire that shapes gold
And makes it more resplendent
More precious

A

Upon the wings
Of a lone seagull
My soul
Will drift over Table mountain
As it soars toward peace

The clouds will be my companions
Hiding the earth from my view
A sea of silence will fill my ears
So friends be assured
Our love and friendship
Will last longer than forever
Behind the wind echoes

Friends
My soul will find peace
Feel renewed strength
Invulnerability

B

Cold winter gales
Throw waves
upon cowering rocks
My heart reaches out
Toward sands
No longer lamenting
Skeleton trees at peace
Still mangled and bleeding
But filled with joy

Similar to my heart
The struggle against the pain
The fight for life
continues
But with a new strength
Now that I feel your touch
Oceans cannot stop heart feelings

A

The tree stands silent
Beneath the moon
Its leaves motionless
Branches heavy
With dreams and darkness
Winds touch it
Disturbing the stillness
The tree yawns
A sentinel thing
Waking from sleep
All motion
A fluid being
All life

From its branches
Breaks forth a soft roar
A voice
Responding to the winds touch
Within the core of myself
Unfamiliar feelings of strength
Energy
My heart wants to shout

Shout
What

B

♫

The leaves turn silver
In the moonlight
A multitude of vivid brightness
The old tree
Something in the wind
And I see your face
Smiling

My soul knows the end of wonder
And enchantment
Illness and pain
Have struck a deep chasm
Between now and then
Hopes and dreams
Have all rumbled away
Into a rainbowed space
This world is hard
Concrete
With reality and pain

There are no iridescent colonnades
Full of moonlight
Standing in lost meadows
No mountains echoing
With the sound of the wind
But there is solace in nature
Love of friends
Sharing all the format
Of life and death

♫

♪

I must accept the fact
Pain is mine to bear
From sunrise to sunset
But there is also strength
To live and work
One day at a time
And courage
To show love for others

Hopefully each day
Another stone
Of anguish and unkind thoughts
Will be lifted
Removed from this world
Enhancing love and life's beauty

Nature
Smiles in spring
Laughs in summer
Yawns in autumn
Rests in winter

Life is difficult and painful
But tears purify the soul
Friends draw hearts closer

♪

ℰ

The dark of night
Shrouds the earth
A flower
Folds its petals in slumber

With the dawn the petals open
Receiving the sunshine
Speckled with darting clouds
The life of a flower is hope
Fulfillment and beauty
Peace and tears

Rain falls
Evaporates
Becomes clouds
And again rain falls
And joins the stream
Wandering towards the sea
The life of clouds
Is one of farewell
Reunion
Tears and friendship
Sorrow and love

ℬ

♄

The soul
Drifts in a world of substance
Passing like clouds
Over valleys of sorrow
Mountains of happiness
Until it meets
The breeze of death
And returns to its beginning
The endless ocean
Of love and friendship

Friends your smile
Dances
Within the sunshine
Spreading comfort
Understanding and love
Your soul
Supports this lonely seagull
With compassion and whispers courage
To the lamenting tide
And comforts my soul

You listened to my touch
And felt the wind echoes

♌

ᘓ

It's my belief
That God permits each soul
To paint sunsets and sunrises
For the joy of loved ones
Left behind

Each dawn and twilight
Someone take up the great palette
Of heavenly hues
And turns the brushes to the sky
There they create
A spectacular sunrise and sunset
Lovingly and carefully etched
And then they wait
With hope
To hear what loved ones will say
When they see the sunset full of love
Painted especially for them

But people are often thoughtless
Too busy
And seldom look up at the sky
And sometimes the painter
Has only the admiration
Of the angels
And seagulls

ᗸ

ℐ

But until the last hue fades
The artist waits
And hopes

In painful darkness
Throughout the night
With fear I draw
Each searing breath

Your warmth is a blessing
It binds the hands
Of a grasping death

You heard my lonely hearts cry
And cared enough to come
With loving friendship
You dry my eyes
And halt the cheerless
Chilling numb of pain

Your bright smile
Gives me strength
Courage to live
One day at a time

ℬ

Night after night
I lay in the dark silences
From this omniscient state
Undetected by the stars
I begin the silent
Motion of composition
This nostalgic flight
With voices from the past

I write
Only for the things left unsaid
I appear one last time
In printed word
Only to say good-bye
You're a cherished part of my soul

Forgive these boring
Idyllic etchings
These wanderings through
The minds' sandcastles
Because they bear the mark
Of a nature love
A naïve sentimental fool

&

Words of love and friendship
Never to be silenced
Precious moments
Lost forever
And all I have left is memory
Give me deliverence
From this nocturnal flight

Friends
Admittedly I didn't know
Exactly what I would say
When I began
But now I'm certain

Before you came to touch my life
Fear and hurt
Cemented strong barriers into my heart
Where no one was ever allowed

With compassion and honesty
Support and understanding
You shattered the walls
Destroyed the barriers
And opened my heart

&

You listened to my touch
And felt the wind echoes

While there is life beneath the sun
Behind the wind echoes
It will hold the love
Of our splendid friendship
We'll always share tears
While someone suffers
And the smiles of a lifetime

I know you'll be with me
In spirit
On my journey
Behind the wind echoes
And one day I'll see you again

The crisis is nearing an end
The battle against cancer
Almost concluded
The living carry on

The words of final embrace
The tears of friendship
The coming home to die

Some bygone afternoon
Fading into a dark night
Life's candle will flicker and die
Friends be assured
Our memories and love
Our friendship
Will last forever
Behind the wind echoes

You listened to my touch
And felt the wind echoes
You walked beside me
Beyond a shadows reach
Behind the wind echoes

With every sunset
A twilight is born
Forever
This lonely seagull
Will cry out with love

♋

Friends
Always listen to a touch
And feel the wind echoes

While there is life
Beneath the sun
Beyond a shadows reach
Our friendship will exist
We'll always share smiles
Hopes and dreams
Behind the wind echoes

When I pass
Beyond a shadows reach
Remember me
With smiles and happiness
Dry the tears
With your hearts' sunshine
Touch the rains teardrops
With your soul

Memories
Friendship
Love
Are longer than eternity

♌

ℰ

Watch the gulls
Vanish into a sunset
And hear the rustle of my soul
Upon their wings
As I bid you farewell

Hear the wind echo
My love for you
And know you're cherished
Longer than forever

Take notice of the seagulls
And ponder this

Seagulls
Are teardrops
With wings

The End and the Beginning

ℬ

Epilogue

It's my belief, family and friends are a richness beyond comprehension. There's something unspoken in a handshake, a friendly smile, a touch, difficult to explain. These friendly gestures are a quiet strength, liken to shimmering sunshine after a rain, the golden harvest of colours in autumn. It echoes words of comfort, soft as a whispering springtime breeze.

I am a member of the Niagara Falls Canada Pilot Club. It is comprised of, what I feel, is the most extraordinary group of ladies I have ever had the pleasure to meet. Trust me when I say this, I have travelled extensively. I have made friends with lions, hippo, elephant, cheetah and many other special animals in Southern Africa. I know about friendship. Have you ever been 'up close and personal' with a wounded lion, in the wilds? I have and it was an amazing experience.

The friendship, laughter and happy closeness of our group overcomes the worst things the world can throw at you. When we are together, a blizzard or tempest could be raging outside, but inside the sun is shining and the room is filled with warmth, sharing and loving friendships.

We recently moved to Village Creek, in rural Stevensville, a quaint little village, near Niagara Falls. Safari Niagara is so close to our home, in the early morning hours we hear the lions roar and the monkeys chatter is so loud, you would think they are in our backyard. Deer are welcome here. They stand in the middle of the road, visiting with each other and know the cars will wait and not disturb them. Everyone in Village Creek has listened to the wind echoes! We are one big, happy family. Whomever we meet while out strolling or driving, always has a happy smile and a friendly wave that shouts: "Hi neighbour! Just call me if you need anything!"

Everyone in Village Creek and in Pilot Club of Niagara have been beyond a shadows reach and brought the beautiful wind echoes to share with anyone in need of a smile, a hug, a friend.

Open your hearts, my friends. It's a small world we live in. Help each other anyway you can. Begin each day with a smile and pass that happiness to everyone who touches your life.

Watch the seagulls in flight. Reach out to them. You will feel them reaching back. Give your heartaches to the seagulls. They will cry out to you with love and change your tears to smiles.

SEAGULLS,
ARE TEARDROPS
WITH WINGS!